We dedicate this book to William H. (Holly) Whyte, who got us started on this extraordinary adventure.

How to Turn a Place Around

A Handbook for Creating Successful Public Spaces

How to Turn a Place Around

A Handbook for Creating Successful Public Spaces

Project for Public Spaces, Inc.

ISBN 0-9706324-0-1

Project for Public Spaces
700 Broadway, 4th floor
New York, NY 10003
www.pps.org
(212) 620-5660
info@pps.org

KATHLEEN MADDEN, WRITER
ANDY WILEY-SCHWARTZ, EDITOR
DESIGNED BY ANN ANTOSHAK

Table of Contents

Project for Public Spaces would like to thank the Laura Jane Musser Fund for helping to make this publication possible.

Foreword

Thirty years ago in New York City, the primary activities of a neighborhood took place in the streets—on stoops and sidewalks, next to fire hydrants, and in empty lots—rather than in the city's parks, markets, or civic spaces, because these more traditional public spaces were either not available or they were in a total state of disrepair. Where people still gathered, they gravitated to the historic places built prior to World War II because the newer public spaces were either non-existent or unusable. It was a sad, deeply disturbing, yet highly motivating time.

We are emerging from that era, though the last half of the 20th century was a devastating time for our cities and communities. The causes were many, but I put most of the blame on urban renewal and suburbanization. These two movements, fueled by the design and engineering professions, focused more on creating objects than on creating good urban spaces that serve people. Moreover, city agencies were not responsive to the holistic needs of their neighborhoods; more often they advanced the agendas of their disciplines and departments (traffic, buildings, etc.) at the expense of creating good urban spaces. As a result, many cherished public places have been destroyed, and opportunities to create new ones have been lost.

Growing up, I witnessed the early results of this devastation, as well as the early environmental activism of people who were looking for alternatives. My personal experience started at Citibank in the 1960s, which at that time, encouraged its employees to volunteer in their communities. I organized the first Earth Day in New York City in 1970 and started the Academy for Black and Latin Education (ABLE), a "street academy" whose community organizers taught high school dropouts literally on the streets, and in the burned-out and vacant buildings where they hung out.

During that time, I had the opportunity to learn from many people who were looking carefully at the uniqueness and strengths of communities: Margaret Mead, the anthropologist; Barbara Ward (Lady Jackson), an international development economist; and William H. (Holly) Whyte, the urbanologist, author, and founder of the Street Life Project. Each of these inspiring individuals was searching for alternative solutions to important urban issues from his or her own perspective. Working with Holly Whyte on the Street Life Project gave me a deep conviction that communities can regenerate themselves by using their own skills; I discovered that public places—parks, plazas, squares, street, bus stops, train stations, and the spaces around neighborhood institutions—can become nexuses around which communities can come together and around which they can mobilize.

Today there is a growing understanding of how a focus on place can change how professionals function. If we move away from our own agendas and toward the idea of creating places, there will be a major shift in how our communities and cities function and grow. In fact, many communities are turning to alternatives to the traditional project-oriented approach to neighborhood revitalization. We are making headway. Downtowns are once again becoming places to walk and shop and gather. Our city parks are greener than at any time since the turn of the last century, and we are discovering new ways for them and for our downtown plazas and civic squares to function as centers of community life.

At Project for Public Spaces, a nonprofit organization I founded in 1975, we have developed what I believe is a unique understanding of the complex social and spatial issues that go into helping citizens to rebuild their communities. As our ideas have crystallized, we have developed a set of diagrams and performance-evaluation methods that help us to understand why some public spaces function and others fail. This book is about those ideas and tools; and by highlighting nearly a dozen examples from our recent experiences in communities around the United States it is intended to help people evaluate any type of public space, from a neighborhood playground to a major tourist attraction.

This book is a collaborative effort representing 25 years of hard work by the many amazing people who have come to work at PPS, but especially those who have stuck around and made this organization what it is today. Our longest-serving staff member, Kathy Madden, is primarily responsible for finally getting down on paper the collective wisdom that we have gathered from the communities we have been working in for the last quarter century. Stephen Davies, our tireless promoter of public markets and sound transportation policy, also contributed greatly to the conceptualization of this book. We hope that everyone who reads this book will learn how to create and improve public spaces in their own communities, and come to appreciate the value of short-term actions and small, yet visible changes. With an understanding of how a place works, we firmly believe that any place can be "turned around."

Fred Kent, *President*
PROJECT FOR PUBLIC SPACES

About Project for Public Spaces

The year 2005 marks the 30th anniversary of Project for Public Spaces as a nonprofit organization offering technical assistance, research, education, planning, and design. PPS's mission is to create and sustain public places that build communities. It operates programs based on transportation, parks, plazas and civic squares, public markets, community institutions, and public buildings. Since the organization's founding in 1975, PPS staff have worked in more than 1,200 communities, both within the U.S. and abroad, to help grow public spaces into vital community places—with programs, uses, and people-friendly settings that highlight local assets, spur social and economic rejuvenation, and serve common needs. In improving these public environments, PPS focuses on creating places that enrich people's experience of public life, through their distinctive identities and their integration into the community fabric.

> "Lowly unpurposeful and random as they may appear, sidewalk contacts are the small change from which a city's wealth of public life may grow."
> JANE JACOBS

BLEECKER STREET, NEW YORK CITY

> "Blank walls proclaim the power of the institution and the inconsequence of the individual, whom they are clearly meant to intimidate."
> WILLIAM H. WHYTE

LOUISIANA STREET, HOUSTON, TEXAS

I. Why "places" are important to cities

Cities in America have begun to look more like each other in recent years, and every place is beginning to look like every other place. Stores, buildings and streets are increasingly homogenous, and traffic dominates our lives, even in small towns. As driving has become the main way for people to get around, walking has become a lost art.

Imagine another kind of city—one in which walking has been rediscovered, and streets and sidewalks invite people to stroll, linger, and socialize—not just move on through. Imagine locally owned businesses with their own character and style, where you know your retailer by name—and a public market offering the freshest locally grown fruit and vegetables. Imagine buildings that aren't interchangeable with those built by some other developer in another town, but whose look and functions are related to their place. Imagine parks and squares that are the highlight of the city, where the community gathers for its civic, cultural and social functions. These are the types of places that come to mind when we think about a livable community.

This book is not about any particular kind of community. It is about every community, because we believe that the same principles apply to dense urban neighborhoods and downtowns as well as to small towns and suburbs, to diverse communities as well as those with a single ethnic group. Each community has the means and the potential to create its own public places.

Critical roles that public places play in communities

Public places are a stage for our public lives. They are the parks where celebrations are held, where marathons end, where children learn the skills of a sport, where the seasons are marked and where cultures mix. They are the streets and sidewalks in front of homes and businesses where friends run into each other and where exchanges both social and economic take place. They are the "front porches" of our public institutions —city halls, libraries, and post offices—where we interact with each other and with government.

need only to walk down the street to find places they cherish. Indeed, great public spaces can be world-renowned, or they can be important because the people in a particular neighborhood value them.

Think about your favorite public space in your everyday life: It might be your neighborhood park, the

Revitalizing streets for walking, gathering, and shopping is perhaps the most direct example of how placemaking can benefit a city or town economically.

When cities and neighborhoods have thriving public spaces, residents have a strong sense of community; conversely, when they are lacking, they may feel less connected to each other.

Places give identity to cities

Without great public places, there would be no great cities. For example, the skating rink and the other public spaces around Rockefeller Center are one of the most-visited tourist attractions in New York City. Thousands gather there for the annual lighting of the holiday tree, or to stand in the street outside the "Today Show" studios, hoping to be on television. These public spaces represent New York the way the Eiffel Tower represents Paris. While people travel thousands of miles to experience such revered places as the Piazza San Marco in Venice, the Champs Elysee in Paris, Central Park in New York, Miami's beaches, or Riverwalk in San Antonio, others

outdoor café where you read the morning paper, or the path you use to stroll around the lake after dinner. These community places are just as important to the identity of cities as their more famous counterparts, because they are where the people who live and work in a community experience their neighborhoods and each other.

Places benefit cities economically

Public spaces have many real and measurable economic benefits. For example, parks can contribute significantly to the land values in a city. In New York, the real estate values around Bryant Park, Central Park, Prospect Park and Riverside Park are the highest in the city. Minneapolis' prime residential areas are located along the extensive park and trail system surrounding its numerous lakes. California's Pacific Coast beaches and parks provide the setting for some of the most expensive homes in the country. In Denver, prices for unfinished lofts in a former flour-mill on the new Platte River Greenway are far above the city's average. Indeed, throughout the country, greenways have become the new type of public space, high-lighted in real estate ads that list houses "on the greenway" as a desirable location.

In New York, the Greenmarket on the north end of Union Square has been a major catalyst in revital-izing the surrounding neighbor-hood. Upscale restaurants in the area buy produce at the Greenmarket and develop their menus around what is fresh season-ally. Following the example of Union Square, 26 additional green-markets are now helping to revital-ize neighborhoods all over New York City. Little Rock, Arkansas' River Market has helped bring the city's downtown to life, spurring development of residential apart-ments, a museum, the relocation of the city's library, and a sports arena. Seattle's Pike Place Market is a major tourist attraction, supporting more than 600 businesses with sales of over $100 million.

Revitalizing streets for walking, gathering, and shopping is perhaps the most direct example of how placemaking can benefit a city or town economically. Too many towns suffer from streets dedicated to moving high volumes of traffic quickly—a goal that effectively elim-inates foot traffic, parking and other features necessary for healthy street life and economic activity. In New Haven, Connecticut, a new streetscape that incorporated wider sidewalks, large trees, enhanced parking, and a community-inspired leasing and development program, helped bring Chapel Street back to life, rejuvenating an important neighborhood in that city.

Places help the environment

Public spaces also have environ-mental benefits because they give relief to urban living. Not only do they reduce the need for and dependence on the automobile, but parks and other "green" public spaces, such as waterfronts and wildlife areas, increase people's appreciation for and stewardship over the natural environment, and also provide habitats for animals. For example, Brooklyn's Prospect Park is home to more than 200 species of birds.

Places provide settings for cultural activities

Often, public places offer free, open forums for people to encounter art and to participate in other cultural activities. From "Shakespeare in the Park" festivals to string quartets on a downtown plaza, good places foster and enhance a city's cultural life. Providence, Rhode Island's WaterFire, an award winning fire and music installation, has had an impressive cultural and eco-nomic impact, attracting hundreds of thousands of visitors to the downtown riverfront on summer and fall evenings. A symbol of the city's renaissance, WaterFire brings people and events to a central urban area that had been deserted after dark.

What makes a place great?

When people describe a place they enjoy, words like "safe," "fun," "charming," and "welcoming" tend to come up repeatedly. These types of adjectives describe the Intangible Qualities—the qualitative aspects—of a particular space. Intangible qualities can be measured quantitatively in a variety of ways, by using existing statistics or by conducting research, although experience has shown that such measurements have their limitations.

CHINATOWN, NEW YORK CITY

In researching more than 1,000 public spaces around the world, we have found four key qualities of successful public spaces: Accessibility, Activities, Comfort, and Sociability.

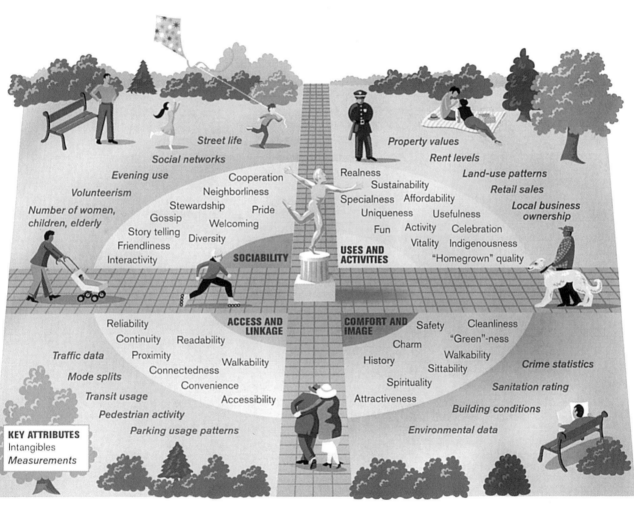

SOCIABILITY

Street life
Social networks
Evening use
Volunteerism
Number of women, children, elderly

Cooperation
Neighborliness
Stewardship   Pride
Gossip
Story telling   Welcoming
Friendliness   Diversity
Interactivity

USES AND ACTIVITIES

Property values
Rent levels
Realness   Land-use patterns
Sustainability
Specialness   Affordability   Retail sales
Uniqueness   Usefulness   Local business
Fun   Activity   Celebration   ownership
Vitality   Indigenousness
"Homegrown" quality

ACCESS AND LINKAGE

Reliability
Continuity   Readability
Traffic data   Proximity
Connectedness   Walkability
Mode splits
Convenience
Transit usage   Accessibility
Pedestrian activity
Parking usage patterns

KEY ATTRIBUTES
Intangibles
Measurements

COMFORT AND IMAGE

Safety   Cleanliness
Charm   "Green"-ness
History   Walkability
Sittability   Crime statistics
Spirituality
Attractiveness   Sanitation rating
Building conditions
Environmental data

ILLUSTRATION: ANNIE BISSETT

Access

A successful public space is easy to get to, and is visible as well. People can easily circulate within it, making it convenient to use different parts of the space. Physical elements can affect access (for instance, a continuous row of shops along a street is more interesting and generally safer to walk by than a blank wall or empty lot), as can perceptions (for example, the ability to see a public space from a distance). Accessible public places have a high turnover in parking, and, ideally, are convenient to public transit.

AMSTERDAM, THE NETHERLANDS

Comfort and Image

Perceptions about safety and cleanliness, the scale of adjacent buildings, and a place's character or charm are often foremost in people's minds in deciding whether to use a place—as are more tangible issues such as having a comfortable place to sit! The importance of giving people the choice to sit where they want is generally underestimated.

LUXEMBOURG GARDENS, PARIS, FRANCE

Uses and Activities

KUNGSTRADGARDEN, STOCKHOLM, SWEDEN

Activities are the basic building blocks of a place. They are the reasons why people come the first time, and why they return. They can also make a place special or unique.

When there is nothing to do there, a place will be empty and unused and that generally means that something is wrong.

Sociability

LAFAYETTE SQUARE, NEW ORLEANS

When people see friends, meet and greet their neighbors, and feel comfortable interacting with strangers, they tend to feel a stronger sense of place or attachment to their community—and to the place that fosters these types of social activities. This makes sociability a difficult but unmistakable quality for a place to achieve.

Why many public spaces fail

Today, many public spaces seem to be intentionally designed to be looked at but not touched. They are neat, clean and empty—as if to say, "no people, no problem!" But when a public space is empty, vandalized, or used chiefly by undesirables, this is generally an indication that something is very wrong with its design, or its management, or both.

The following pairs of photographs illustrate some of the most common problems of public spaces.

"It is difficult to design a space that will not attract people. What is remarkable is how often this has been accomplished." WILLIAM H. WHYTE

Some problems are related to the design of a space:

Lack of good places to sit

Many public spaces don't provide even a place to sit. So, in their very protracted quest to just be comfortable, people are often forced to adapt to the situation in their own way.

SHELL OIL BUILDING, HOUSTON, TEXAS

Sometimes they have to sit on their briefcases.

SHELL OIL BUILDING, HOUSTON, TEXAS

Lack of gathering points

Gathering points can be features people want or need, such as playgrounds, or they can be places where elements—a bus stop, vending cart, or outdoor seating—combine to create a focal point. This Paris park forces people to sit in unsociable ways, and asks them *not* to climb on the sculpture.

PARC DE LA VILLETTE, PARIS

Though located along a stretch of the Pacific Coast Highway, this California park has loads of activities, food, and places to sit. It is a busy, healthy gathering place.

LAGUNA BEACH, CALIFORNIA

Poor entrances and visually inaccessible spaces

A dark or narrow entrance such as this one keeps people out instead of inviting them in.

BRYANT PARK, NEW YORK CITY

The same entrance, redesigned to be inviting and open. The kiosks sell coffee and sandwiches, and the interior of the park is visible from the street.

BRYANT PARK, NEW YORK CITY

Dysfunctional features

Often features are designed simply to punctuate a space. They are more visual than functional.

PARC DIAGONAL MAR, BARCELONA, SPAIN

Good features such as this friendly gorilla, encourage activity to occur around them.

BERLIN ZOO, GERMANY

Paths that don't go where people want to go

PHOENIX, ARIZONA

Paths that lead nowhere
are useless.

LUXEMBOURG GARDENS, PARIS, FRANCE

There is an art to making
a path that pulls people
along it, or allows them to
stop and relax.

Some problems are the result of poor management or no management of the space:

Domination of a place by vehicles

A main street is not a highway. One should not fear crossing the street, on foot or in a car.

PARIS, FRANCE

Crossing the street should be an easy comfortable activity.

LAGUNA BEACH, CALIFORNIA

Blank walls or dead zones around the edges of a place

VERONA, ITALY

Having a thriving, active area around a space is as important to its success as the design and management of the space itself.

COPENHAGEN, DENMARK

This blank wall contributes nothing to the activity of the street. In fact, it doesn't even look real.

Inconveniently located transit stops

Transit stops located in places where no one will ever use them are a good recipe for failure.

SAN ANTONIO, TEXAS

A transit stop in a busy, active place can make that place even better, as well as increase transit use.

CHRISTCHURCH, NEW ZEALAND

Nothing going on

CITY HALL PLAZA, BOSTON, MASSACHUSETTS

A lack of programs and activities such as outdoor films, a market, or street festivals can make for an empty, forlorn plaza or space.

PRAGUE, CZECH REPUBLIC

This square in Prague is full of life, in part due to constant programs and the availability of food.

II. An alternative approach to planning public spaces

Why don't we have better public spaces in America today?

With all of the traveling people do, visiting other "places"—from Disneyland's Main Street to Aspen, Colorado—one has to ask a seemingly obvious question: Why don't we have more and better public places in our own communities? Think about the parks, main streets, bus stops and public buildings in your community, and think about how those places could be more inviting, friendlier, or easier to use. You probably have lots of ideas—how traffic lights could be timed better, where crosswalks and benches should be, what a good bus shelter would look like.

Now think about the last time anyone asked you for those ideas and then has done something to help you realize your vision. Never happened, did it? But you probably can remember when the city has introduced a new "project" to you—a stadium, convention center, shopping mall or highway bypass—and asked you to come to a meeting to tell them what you thought about it.

This is what we call the project-oriented approach to planning. Used by most cities, this approach usually does not work if you're aiming to create great public spaces. Not to say that "projects" aren't good for communities—because they can be. But a project usually comes about because of a political situation, or a capital budget, or because some developer has made a proposal to the city. A project rarely comes out of a discussion with a community about how to create good public places within that community. The unfortunate reality is that no one is in charge of the public spaces in any city in America today. If cities are going to become better places to live, the quality of these places must be addressed directly and aggressively, using a very different approach than is being used today.

versus bottom-up: Basically, it's upside down!

A typical scenario might go something like this: A town council has decided to build a community center in a neighborhood park. While it is true that some type of community center will fill an important need in that neighborhood, this is a project of the council, rather than a community-driven

The unfortunate reality is that no one is in charge of the public spaces in any city in America today.

The current approach to planning cities is "project-driven" and "discipline-based." It is where the project (that new stadium, courthouse, or light rail system) is the reason for the action. Professionals develop alternative design schemes and take them to "the community," which reviews the project and provides input into which scheme should be selected. What's the problem with this approach? It does not begin with anything that the community has defined as an issue, and it does not start with a public space. This approach is top-down

action. This approach leaves the local residents with no opportunity to bring up issues they are concerned about—such as the safety of their children, who, even now, can't ride their bikes to the park because of the dangerous traffic on surrounding streets. As a result, important issues are left unaddressed. The local traffic engineer isn't even aware that he should be looking at ways to slow traffic and improve pedestrian and bicycle safety. A couple of years later a community center is built. But children do not use it nearly as much as they might,

Two approaches to planning public spaces	
Current approach	**Alternative approach**
Project-driven	Place-driven
Discipline-based	Community-based

because it is difficult to cross the busy surrounding streets.

Four issues contribute to this upside–down approach to creating public spaces:

1. **The community is not approached until it's too late.** Their input is, in effect, "after the fact:" The ideas have already been developed and the community is really just being asked to react to ideas, rather than talk about what their concerns are.

2. **The community's strengths** its knowledge of local issues and its unique insights about how an area currently functions—are not being tapped at a critical point: the beginning. Instead they are asked to review a plan, a task that can be overwhelming, even for an expert. Seeing all of the material that has been prepared, all at once—which represents a great deal of effort—makes it difficult to give input.

3. **Timing.** Projects take a long time to come to fruition, whereas smaller "improvements" can happen much more quickly, and often with less expense.

4. **Lack of communication.** Several city agencies, such as the departments of transportation, planning, and parks, deal with different community concerns—but they work alone, rather than

collaborating with each other to create holistic, more effective projects.

Why not try a different approach?

A fairly radical change is needed from the way that communities are currently being planned. The planning process needs to begin by talking and working with the community. This approach starts with the professionals eliciting the community's ideas—their concerns, but more importantly their ideas for changes to their local public spaces. People can be brought together in meetings or in a workshop where they evaluate their local spaces and then discuss the issues and form their vision. Simple (and sometimes more complex) observations can also be made to show how people actually use the spaces in their communities. All of the information that evolves from the meetings, surveys, observations, etc. is a what a community envisions for its future, and it is what needs to be addressed to make sure that the community's vision is realized as soon as possible. The professionals' role then becomes implementing the vision of the community.

III. Principles of creating great places

Over the years, we have come to understand that there are principles that guide our work. When applied to any successful revitalization effort, they form a sort of narrative thread that runs through the process. The principles cover the importance of a community's vision for creating their own places, the difference between creating a "place" versus a design, the important role of experimentation and management in sustaining any successful space, among others.

The principles outlined on the following pages represent our view of what it takes to develop and manage a successful place. We have illustrated each principle with an example from our experience. Not every one is a success, nor is every example one that couldn't have happened without us. However, each case study provides a snapshot of a community, working together to create a better neighborhood, city, or quality of life.

UNDERLYING IDEAS

1 The community is the expert

2 You are creating a place— not a design

3 You can't do it alone

4 They always say it can't be done

PLANNING AND OUTREACH TECHNIQUES

5 You can see a lot just by observing

6 Develop a vision

TRANSLATING IDEAS INTO ACTION

7 Form supports function

8 Triangulate

IMPLEMENTATION

9 Start with the petunias

10 Money is not the issue

11 You are never finished

1 The community is the expert

People provide perspective and valuable insights into how an area functions; they have a unique understanding of the issues that are important. The sooner the community becomes involved in the planning process the better—ideally before any planning has been done. And people should be encouraged to stay involved throughout the improvement effort so that they become owners or stewards of the place as it evolves.

The Importance of the Ordinary Citizen in Creating Good Public Spaces

In order to create a successful place, it's essential to find a way to uncover people's talents and then incorporate them into the process in a meaningful way. Tapping into the ideas and talents of the community is crucial in deciding what will be done to improve an existing place, or in developing a vision for a new place.

The people who live or work near a place know from experience which areas are dangerous and why, which spaces are comfortable, where the traffic moves too fast, and where their children can safely walk or bike or play. As our friend Jody Kretzmann says, "No community on the face of the Earth has ever been built except on the skills and resources and contributions of the gifts of the people who live there." Unfortunately, residents are rarely

Case Study: Friends of Mount Vernon Place, Baltimore, Maryland

Residents of the Mount Vernon neighborhood in Baltimore were concerned about the state of Mount Vernon Place: a four–block, historic park that was not well used, maintained, or managed. Almost 100 residents turned out to a meeting in April, 1999, where we helped them to evaluate the existing uses of Mount Vernon Place, and come up with a vision for what the park could become in the future.

The result was a series of both short– and long–term ideas that included the formation of Our Front Yard, a working group of residents that has continued to meet every two weeks to strategize the revitalization of Mount Vernon Place. In order to reach a wider public constituency, Our Front Yard changed its name to Friends of Mount Vernon Place and became a tax–exempt nonprofit organization. The group's mission is the "revitalization of Mount Vernon Park and the creation of a polite, public place enabling current and future residents and visitors to enjoy the wealth of cultural resources, natural beauty, and historic significance of Mount Vernon Place."

In little more than a year, the Friends applied for and received a grant to hire a local high school student to help maintain Mount Vernon Place over a summer; got the park onto Baltimore's "priority list" for maintenance and beautification; formed alliances with the Mount Vernon Cultural District and the neighborhood–based Mount Vernon Belvedere Association; organized several volunteer park clean–up days; and participated in a flower mart and book festival in the park. Most important, they wrote a $2.8 million proposal to develop and implement a master plan for the park. "We're not a huge group – our paid membership is 67 individuals and 7 institutions," says Helen Schlossberg Cohen, a Friends co–chairperson. "But we definitely believe in the power of our community. We all have ideas about preserving what we have here at Mount Vernon Place, and what we'd like to see in the future."

> "We definitely believe in the power of our community. We all have ideas about preserving what we have here at Mount Vernon Place, and what we'd like to see in the future."
>
> HELEN COHEN, *Co-Chair, Friends of Mount Vernon Place*

MT. VERNON PLACE, BALTIMORE, MARYLAND

asked to contribute this information to the planning process. All too often, people's knowledge and resources are totally wasted. Just imagine how much human knowledge and experience is lost everyday because we haven't figured out how to use it in a meaningful way.

Who is "the community?"

"The community" is anyone who has an interest or stake in a particular place. It is made up of the people who live near a particular place (whether they use it or not), own businesses or work in the area, or attend institutions such as schools and churches there. It also includes elected officials who represent the area and groups that organize activities there, such as a bocce club or a merchants' association.

To be most effective in creating a public space, the community should form a working group comprised of people who represent entities broader than themselves—for example, a representative of a block or merchants association, a pastor or minister, or the head of development or community affairs for a corporation or institution. These people operate not just from personal interest, but also function as liaisons to their respective groups. We rarely find that existing government bodies, such as city councils can serve as a working group alone.

Betsy Rogers, the woman who turned around New York's Central Park, told us that "There is no one more precious than what I call 'the zealous nut,' the person who really, really loves the community, who lives there and understands what the place means—that is a very precious individual. And that precious individual of course is connected to other individuals, and I think that is the way we begin a dialogue and have an energy source that will propel a project." ■

"No community on the face of the Earth has ever been built except on the skills and resources and contributions of the gifts of the people who live there."
JODY KRETZMANN, ABCD Institute

2 You are creating a place—not a design

Today, there is more and more discussion about the importance of "places." Travel books are devoted to the best "places" in different cities, states and parts of the world. Other books have re-introduced us to the importance of the "places" where we go just to hang out or

stroll when we're not at home or working—or shopping! Many books say that we are losing our "sense of place" and that we need to work very hard to get them back if our communities are to become more livable. Design magazines give awards to projects that they consider the best public space designs. Yet rarely do these award-winning designs turn out to be good "places." Somehow the discussions about the loss of places and the reality of being able to create them have not come together in any meaningful way.

How to create a "place" that is not a design

The central question is "what is the role of design in creating a place?"

From our experience, placemaking requires a radically different approach than is used by most designers today. In contrast to the traditional design or planning process, a place-oriented approach is necessarily broader than one that is primarily design driven. Creating a place depends more on effective management than it does design and requires the involvement of many different disciplines because of the extremely complex issues that need to be addressed. For example, good maintenance and effective security are obviously important but so is good access by foot and public transportation. Amenities such as comfortable seating, well located waste receptacles, effective signage, bathrooms, opportunities to buy

Case Study: Post Office, Montpelier, Vermont

The post office is one of the most important places in downtown Montpelier, drawing people from all over Central Vermont during the week. Unfortunately, it is also the most "unfriendly" building in town. Set back 20 feet from the sidewalk and surfaced with reflective glass, this federally owned building is surrounded by a small landscaped area that keeps people away. Although this is one of the few green areas in the vicinity, it does not invite people to linger; rather, one community member described it as "off-putting." The General Services Administration, the Federal agency that acts as the building's landlord, asked us to help facilitate a community workshop to determine how the post office could fit in better with the community and how it could be more supportive to the downtown life of Montpelier. Using the techniques in this book, we helped the community evaluate the site and they came up with a vision for creating a downtown "place" in and around the post office very quickly.

> The ideas was to create a 'front porch' in front of the post office with rocking chairs and benches, a community bulletin board, a coffee cart, a dog hitch, new cross walks, and traffic-calming devices to improve and encourage pedestrian access to the area.

When the group first looked at the building they simply thought it needed a façade improvement. But when they began to focus on the street level, they realized that they could basically make the upper part of the building disappear—by focusing people's attention on a variety of uses and activities on the ground floor, where they felt they could create a community place. The idea was to create a "front porch" in front of the library with rocking chairs and benches, a community bulletin board, a coffee cart, a dog hitch, new cross walks, and traffic-calming devices to improve and encourage pedestrian access to the area. They also recommended relocating an existing farmer's market closer to the post office to create an additional draw on weekends. With these low-cost improvements, brainstormed in the winter of 2000, the Montpelier community created a place—not a design.

POST OFFICE, MONTPELIER, VERMONT

food etc. are all important qualities of successful places. And it is beyond the experience of any one profession to deal with all of these issues.

There is very little training in how to create places. Schools don't train students to create places. They teach them to design or to build or to study behavior, but not how to use their professional training to tap into the creativity of the community, to help them to create a vision, and to function as a resource in implementing that vision. What we really need is a new national training program in creating good places.

In the meantime, we need to redefine our mission when it comes to public space design. If the new mission is to "create a successful well-used place" then the role of the professionals, including the design professional, is as a resource for communities. They would work with others, such as non-profit organizations and government agencies, to implement the community's vision. In most cases, this means that professionals (or agencies) need to reverse their current role in relation to communities and rather than lead, become supportive to the process.

The way to begin is to just follow these steps:

- **Meet with community representatives** from both public and private sectors to identify the range of issues that the various groups face regarding a particular place.

- **Formulate hypotheses about issues** that merit further data collection and develop a workplan for how to collect this information.

- **Collect the data** that you need to better understand the situation.

- Analyze data, review community input, and **identify potential ideas** for implementation.

- **Conduct a public forum** for community representatives and interested members of the larger community at which you present issues, get feedback and develop, with the community, a vision for the space.

- Translate the results of the meetings and the observations into an **outline of issues and a conceptual plan** that reflects the community's vision.

- **Refine and discuss** these recommendations with the community.

- Develop an **implementation strategy.**

- Develop **design ideas that reflect the vision** and the implementation strategy. ∎

What we really need is a new national training program in creating good places.

3 You can't do it alone

A good public space requires more than any one individual or organization can offer. Partners contribute innovative ideas, and additional financial resources such as in-kind goods and services, or volunteers to help with maintenance or short-term improvement projects. Partners also help to broaden the impact of a project by participating in activities such as joint programming, marketing, fundraising, and security. A strong partnership can also move a project forward by giving it political clout.

The most obvious partners are the people and institutions that are located around a space. They have a major impact on whether a public space will be used and how it will be maintained. The outer "edges" of the public space are inextricably entwined with the "inner," or actual public space: each is dependent on the other for its success. If the outer edges of a public space include a diverse neighborhood with a range of institutions that all feel connected to the space, then people will have a reason to come to the area both during the day and in the evening, on weekdays and weekends. If there's nothing going on at the edges of a place, however, there's no reason for anyone to come either to the public space or the area around it.

The "edges" of a space provide many partners: schools, churches, libraries, museums, and businesses, among others. The "obvious"

Case study: Maplewood Concierge Company, Maplewood, New Jersey

In the early '90s, New Jersey Transit embarked on a plan to make its train stations into catalysts for the revitalization of the communities around them, as many of the stations were underused. After interviewing people at the Maplewood train station and nearby retailers, we realized that even though Main Street was only a block away from the station, transit riders were too rushed to shop. This fact was as frustrating for the merchants as it was for the commuters. We suggested a partnership between New Jersey Transit and local Maplewood businesses, in which a "concierge" operation was established to provide products and services to transit passengers at the station. Located at an oak counter in the Maplewood Station, a concierge represents nearly 70 local businesses, from car repair to take–home dinners, serving the 2,000 commuters who leave before or return after these businesses are closed.

> Even though Main Street was only a block away from the station, transit riders were too rushed to shop.

NJ Transit worked with the local chamber to contact area retailers, whose shares in the for–profit concierge company allow them to provide services to patrons. Customers place orders in the morning, in person, or by fax, and pick them up in the evening at the train station, for a 10% surcharge. Service providers, such as accountants, insurance agents, and housing contractors, use the concierge to attract new customers. Transit agencies from other parts of New Jersey, Chicago, Baltimore, even Tokyo and Berlin have expressed interest in starting their own version of the Maplewood Concierge Company.

MAPLEWOOD, NEW JERSEY

partners are people who own the space or who already have a vested interest in it. For example, if a space is located downtown, perhaps near city hall or a library, these institutions are logical partners to be approached by the parks department or a group that wants to improve the space. The edges of a space can suggest other partners as well: Residents, workers in nearby offices or retail establishments, members of churches or cultural or civic institutions, and students all are potential partners.

"Unlikely" partners

Look for "unlikely" partners as well: those who may not come immediately to mind because they are not located adjacent to the space, but who could be interested in it for a variety of other reasons. For example, it could give them a visibility or presence in the area that they wouldn't otherwise have.

Different partners emerge at different stages of a project. The "obvious partners" should be involved early on as part of the group that defines the issues and conducts some of the initial observations, whereas other "unlikely partners" (traffic departments, government agencies, etc.) will emerge as the project moves forward and a vision develops. For example, a downtown organization, in conjunction with the city, may initiate an effort to improve a space. As the process moves forward, partners such as a botanical garden, museum, or conservatory may become involved. Or a transit agency may have transportation funds to enhance bus stops as focal points of the system. ∎

The edges of a space can suggest other partners as well: residents, workers in nearby offices or retail establishments, members of churches or cultural or civic institutions, and students all are potential partners.

4 They always say, "It can't be done"

The professionals responsible for activities that directly affect public spaces—such as planning, traffic and transit, recreation, and education—have roles that are peripheral to those spaces. Therefore, when an idea stretches beyond the reach of an organization, people are often told, "It can't be done." But when officials say, "It can't be done," often what they really mean is: "We've never done things that way before."

Government is compartmentalized. As a result, people working in government are limited in their ability to deal with public spaces effectively. While separate agencies address a myriad of issues, no city in the United States has a department or person responsible for the development and management of public places.

What are the obstacles?

Bureaucratic roadblocks

In some communities, people report that everything they think of doing to improve their public spaces is illegal. For example, some cities prohibit eating and drinking on public sidewalks, which prevents the liveliness and fostered by the sidewalk café. Similarly, vending carts, an important ingredient for success in many public spaces, are still illegal in many places because of old sanitation laws from the 19th century. Some laws are even more prohibitive of public life. One city outlawed outdoor chess tables because the activity was considered to be "gaming;" elsewhere, a petting zoo was prohibited at a farmers market because it

Case Study: Monroe Street, Tallahassee, Florida

People who worked and owned businesses in downtown Tallahassee, Florida had a problem. Vehicles on Monroe Street sometimes reached speeds of 55 mph through the heart of downtown—so fast they didn't even see the few businesses that were left. People who worked downtown rarely walked anywhere because crossing the street was dangerous, and retailers complained that speeding traffic was a major disincentive for motorists to stop and shop. Even the chief of police was angry, because he continually had to ticket people who were speeding, which he felt made him into the "bad guy."

> "Some of our police officers are now believers in traffic-calming devices. And there's been a change in the way people act: Drivers are actually more courteous."
> MARILYN LARSON, *Tallahassee Downtown Improvement Authority*

One very simple way of slowing down traffic, and increasing parking at the same time, is to change parking on the street from a parallel structure to angled parking. We suggested this "quick fix" to the residents of Tallahassee. However, because Monroe Street was also officially a state highway, the traffic engineers told the downtown community that angled parking was something that simply could not be done. Unwilling to take no for an answer, the business community, under the leadership of the Tallahassee Downtown Improvement Authority, went to the governor to seek help in obtaining the right to experiment with angled parking. In October 1994, the Florida DOT replaced 53 existing parallel parking spaces with 73 angled spaces. The results were so positive that the project, intended as a six-month demonstration, became permanent. In addition to slower traffic speeds, traffic volume actually increased, further reducing vehicle speeds, making the area safer for pedestrians and thereby attracting more foot traffic. Moreover, reports Marilyn Larsen, head of the Downtown Improvement Authority, "Some of our police officers are now believers in traffic-calming devices. And there's been a change in the way people act: Drivers are actually more courteous!"

Against all odds, the downtown Tallahassee community succeeded in doing what everyone said couldn't be done. After the success on Monroe Street, other area streets were converted from parallel to angled parking as well. Now the Florida DOT, in part because of its positive experience in Tallahassee, is working to calm traffic and build communities and main streets throughout the state.

MONROE STREET, TALLAHASSEE, FLORIDA (BEFORE)

MONROE STREET, TALLAHASSEE, FLORIDA (AFTER)

was illegal to separate an animal from its mother.

One recent solution to such roadblocks is the Business Improvement District (BID), which provides a means of cutting through bureaucracy, and establishing a sense of control. Another, less typical solution is to create a "bureau-cracy–free zone" for an area in which experiments are allowed and in fact encouraged.

Unwillingness to change one's mission

If the mission is to create places in communities, the government offi-cials working in our neighborhoods need to apply their skills to that mission. For example, the tradition-al "safety and mobility" goals of a transportation engineer may be at odds with the development of lively public spaces in many downtowns. While their mission is to move traf-

"If they say it can't be done, it doesn't always work out that way." YOGI BERRA

Narrowly defined responsibilities

Whereas a community's needs are holistic and broad, government serv-ices are focused and narrow. And even though people in government could potentially take on the impor-tant responsibility of creating public spaces, the innate structure and com-partmentalization of government today does not often jibe with the needs of communities. Seattle is the only city that we know of whose gov-ernment has been restructured to address this issue. The city has creat-ed a Department of Neighborhoods, whose mission is to bring a more holistic approach to neighborhood planning, preservation, and develop-ment. Jim Diers, director of the Department, says, "In Seattle, we rec-ognize that what really makes the city work are our neighborhoods. They are the city's strongest assets, along with the active citizens who are part of those neighborhoods."

fic quickly and efficiently through an area, retailers, developers and downtown boosters want the same traffic to slow down, and are contin-ually devising ways to get people out of their cars to walk and shop. However, the transportation profes-sion, like many others, is showing receptiveness to new ideas. Recently, some transportation offi-cials have adopted a new set of values for what is becoming known as "context–sensitive design"—that is, ensuring that transportation projects are created to work harmo-ny with communities.

So when someone says, "It can't be done," reply that, "Maybe it hasn't been done – yet." And keep on working! ∎

5 You can see a lot just by observing

When you observe a space, you learn about how it is actually used, rather than how you think it is used, whether the "place" is a small neighborhood park, a bus stop, or a train station used by thousands of people each day. Observations enable you to quantify what would otherwise be regarded as intuition or opinion.

By recording or mapping the ways people use spaces, you can also learn a lot about what they want from a space. In fact, people will often go to extraordinary lengths to use a space in a particular way. For example, we have seen people use waste receptacles as seats, for sorting their bills, and for cooking clams. Often their actions speak louder than their words.

Public spaces can be observed in many ways: by recording activity in the space at different times of the day and week, by tracing routes people take through it, or by counting people and things during certain events or in certain areas. Many different items can be counted— people, cars, bicycles, baby strollers, even pets! You can also note the traces of past activities in a space

Yogi Berra said, "You can see a lot by observing." He might have added that you can also "hear a lot by listening." Anyone can learn an amazing amount about a public space by observing what happens in and around it, and by listening to the people who use it.

Case study: Bryant Park, New York, New York

Today it is one of the best urban parks in the country, but in the early '80s Bryant Park, located in Midtown Manhattan, was overrun with drug dealers. Fearing for their safety, and put off by the park's high hedges, dingy appearance, and lack of activities, the many office employees and tourists who walked by Bryant Park never ventured in. In order to understand the problems of the space, and to separate reality from perception, we needed to understand how the park was actually used. To do this, we "mapped" the location of all activities both positive and negative, and interviewed people who were using the park. Most revealing was the fact that negative activities such as drug dealing were occurring near the park entrances, as they were very constricted and dark, and it was difficult for people to see past them into the park.

> There was nothing for people to do in the park except sit in dark areas under trees where other people were sleeping and hanging out. There was no place to buy food, no events to act as a draw.

Another important realization was that there was nothing for people to do in the park except sit in dark areas under trees where other people were sleeping and hanging out. There was no place to buy food, no events to act as a draw. While actual crime statistics in the park were, in fact, very low, the perception of crime was quite the opposite. Interviews showed that people from nearby office buildings felt threatened by the drug dealers in the park and were therefore afraid to use it. The dealers, meanwhile, told us that if people didn't want to buy drugs they didn't have to—but they were dominating the space.

Our design recommendations included enlarging the park entrances and removing shrubbery that prevented people from seeing into the park. Two kiosks were installed at the main entrance, with the intention of replacing existing "retail" activity with a different type: snacks and sandwiches. Small green bistro chairs were scattered throughout the park so that people could sit wherever they wanted. A management entity, the Bryant Park Development Corporation, planned activities such as outdoor movies, and a set up a small cart to loan chess and checkers games to park users. A restaurant and small cafe were built at the back of the park, an area that had felt isolated and was particularly unused. The park now functions extremely well as a busy and safe oasis in the heart of Manhattan.

BRYANT PARK, NEW YORK CITY (BEFORE)

BRYANT PARK, NEW YORK CITY (AFTER)

through littered areas or paths that people have worn into grassy areas. If you have the right equipment, time–lapse photography and video-taping can not only collect information, but also have the advantage of providing effective visual results.

Interviewing tells you how people perceive a public space is used, or why they use it in a particular way. Interviews can vary from a few informal questions as part of a conversation to a longer, more formalized survey. Both are valuable and serve different purposes. Storytelling is also a good way to learn about how people use public spaces and what factors repel them, what causes people to interact with a space or with each other, and why they avoid certain spaces. ■

We have seen people use waste receptacles as seats, for sorting their bills, and for cooking clams. Often their actions speak louder than words.

CARL SCHURZ PARK, NEW YORK CITY

Observing the observers: These benches should be double-sided to allow people to see the view *and* watch passersby.

⑥ Develop a vision

A vision for a public space essentially concerns the activities that happen in it. It follows, then, that a vision for a place should be defined by people who live and work around it, rather than by professionals or government entities. We have found that every community has numerous people whose ideas can evolve into a "vision" for a place. One of the ways professionals can help bring forth these ideas

is simply to ask people to think about other places they have been to and enjoyed, and then explore with them the activities that occur in that place and the physical elements that support them. Pictures of successful spaces (and even unsuccessful ones) are a good way of going into more depth about the activities (or lack thereof) in a space, but can also illustrate physical elements, character, types of management, and so forth. Additional insights can be gleaned about the use of existing spaces from observing, interviewing and talking to people.

Our experience in working with communities is that the vision for a particular place can emerge quickly. A community's vision is generally very realistic and practical, yet also filled with innovative ideas; this is because the input is much broader than if the vision were to be generated by just one individual, profession or city agency. A

"Where there is no vision the people perish." Proverbs 29:18

Case Study: Hyde Park Public Square, Fort Worth, Texas

Though Fort Worth, Texas had no "civic heart," its people had enough of a sense of community to understand that something needed to be done about that. In 1999, we helped facilitate an amazing workshop, in which stakeholders in the area around City Hall came together to determine how they could improve the public areas in front of their buildings, and also create a great public place for downtown Fort Worth. These stakeholders included workers from city hall, a Federal office building, a state courthouse, a few privately owned buildings under redevelopment, the convention center, a church, and the headquarters of a major utility company. The initial vision that resulted from these meetings was of a major new public square: a place where people who worked in nearby buildings could come together, and that would bring a strong identity to an area that had none.

Technology was an important tool in evolving that initial vision and getting participation from a much broader community. The city planning department created a website for the project that included descriptions and photos of the history of the area and some potential activities for the square. Local employees received email about the website, and were given suggestions of ways for them to get involved in the project planning. One important—yet easy—way was to answer an online survey about the character of the space, its uses, and its activities. This "idea survey" helped in developing a concept for programming for the new square, which, at the community's request, will include spaces that appeal to all generations, transit access and options, live entertainment, lots of seating (and much of it in the shade), food and flower vendors, and public art and fountains that promote interaction. "You have to show people the possibilities—that's real important," says Elaine Petrus, a community volunteer who has worked on other projects downtown. "Some people have a vision of what they want, but others, that's not what they pay attention to in life. If you show them something, it gets them going with their own ideas."

> "You have to show people the possibilities—that's real important...Some people have a vision of what they want, but others, that's not what they pay attention to in life. If you show them something, it gets them going with their own ideas."
> ELAINE PETRUS,
> *Community Volunteer*

PROPOSED SITE FOR NEW SQUARE, FORT WORTH, TEXAS

community's vision also has many short-term ideas for implementation because people who live or work in a place want to see results much more than people with an arm's-length involvement with a community.

When there is no vision for a space, the community loses because inevitably others, in an effort to "improve" the space, will try things that will probably not be what the community wants to happen. For example, a traffic engineer may widen a road when the community is concerned that there is already too little space for pedestrians, or an empty lot will become a development site when the neighborhood needs a small park or a place for a farmers market.

Essential to the process of developing a vision is the professional's role in facilitating its implementation. From this perspective, **the primary characteristics of a vision for a public place are:**

- A mission or **statement of goals;**

- A definition of **how a space will be used** and by whom;

- Statement of the **character** of the space;

- A conceptual idea of how the space could be **designed;**

- **Models or examples** of similar spaces or parts of those spaces. ■

A community's vision is generally very realistic and practical, yet also filled with innovative ideas; this is because the input is much broader than if is the vision were to be generated by just one individual, profession, or city agency.

7 Form supports function

Although design is a critical ingredient in creating public spaces, the most successful spaces grow out of an understanding of how the community will use the space. We are convinced that if the principles outlined in this book are followed, one will not only begin the design process with a deeper sense of what a place can become, but also enrich that process with better, more creative ideas. Drawing on the talents and vision of the community does not mean foregoing a strong design statement—often, that process contributes to the strength of the project.

Open-space design by architects or landscape designers is typically (though not always) an intellectual exercise in what that individual believes will appear to be beautiful or attractive. It is not usually based on the activities or uses that space should or could support. The reality is that in most cases, it is not until after a space is built that much thought is given to how people will use it. In fact, a good deal of retro-fitting goes on in failed public spaces simply because the function was never seriously considered at the outset. In this respect, we believe that the designer, by following and incorporating the needs articulated by the community, can ultimately make the design of the space more attractive, more interesting to look at and be in—because it will be used.

There are several key steps we

Case study: Rockefeller Center, New York, New York

Rockefeller Center is one of the most popular public spaces in New York—maybe in the entire United States. The Center's Channel Gardens, where the New York City Christmas tree has been lighted every holiday season for over 50 years, extend from the well–known skating rink to Fifth Avenue. A simple example of "form supports function" grew out of a problem that Rockefeller Center's management was having with the planters in the gardens in the mid–1970s: people were sitting on the edges of them and crushing the plants. Rejecting the initial idea of embedding "spikes" in the top of the planters to keep people from sitting on them, the management decided at our suggestion to add wooden benches around the planters to accommodate—and encourage—the desire to sit in the area. This small action protected the plants and accommodated the visitors, and has grown to represent the general approach of Rockefeller Center management toward design issues: encourage use and activity, and keep the area beautiful.

> Rejecting the initial idea of embedding 'spikes' in the top of the planters to keep people from sitting on them, the management decided at our suggestion to add wooden benches around the planters to accommodate— and encourage—the desire to sit in the area.

ROCKEFELLER CENTER, NEW YORK CITY (BEFORE)

ROCKEFELLER CENTER, NEW YORK CITY (AFTER)

have found useful in developing a plan for a space that will be enlivened by various functions.

- **Clarify the program** of uses or functions that are to occur in the space.

- **Diagram how those uses and functions will interrelate** within the space. A good way to do this is by making a "uses and activities" diagram that incorporates pictures of other places.

- **Develop a design that reflects and supports the functions and the character as defined by the community.**

- **Think big** (overall character) **and small** (where will people sit).

- **Study and learn from other successful places.**

Remaining committed to the community's vision and translating that into a well-functioning space is clearly the challenge. We believe that by meeting it, some extraordinary new forms for both public spaces and buildings can emerge. On one hand, it involves allowing the community's views and knowledge to come forth; on the other hand one must learn the skills to understand how spaces function. ■

LUXEMBOURG GARDENS, PARIS, FRANCE

"People tend to sit where there are places to sit. . . The most attractive fountains, the most striking designs, cannot induce people to come and sit if there is no place to sit. Ideally, sitting should be physically comfortable— benches with backrests, well-contoured chairs. It's more important, however, that it be socially comfortable."
WILLIAM H. WHYTE

8 Triangulate

Triangulation, when used as a technique for planning public spaces, means locating elements in a way that greatly increases the chances of activity occurring around them. The idea is to situate them so that the use of each builds off the other. For example, a bench, a trash receptacle and a telephone placed near each other at a bus stop, or the entrance to a market or park, create synergy because there are more chances for activity than if the element were isolated. Another example: If a children's reading room in a new library is located adjacent to a playground in a park with a food kiosk, more activity will occur than if these facilities were sited separately.

Sometimes triangulation occurs spontaneously, for example, on a busy urban street corner where there is something of interest—say, one of the life-size fiberglass cow sculptures painted by artists and set up on the streets of various cities as a public art project. The cows created an excuse for people who didn't know each other to talk to one another. Farmers' markets are also good places to spot examples of triangulation: You can always find perfect strangers chatting about the attributes of and recipes for everything from sweet corn to Japanese eggplants to Jersey tomatoes.

Case study: Chapel Street, New Haven, Connecticut

Chapel Street, once a bustling Main Street in New Haven, Connecticut, had fallen into disrepair and neglect. Turning to professional designers for a solution, property owners were told that a "streetscape plan" was needed: kiosks, benches, and other types of street furniture. One proposal showed new trees that would have blocked shop windows along the street, which didn't please the already struggling retailers.

> "The whole thing is like a mosaic. Each piece needs to be carefully considered: street furniture, flower boxes, a particular tenant for a storefront, tree plantings. If it's done right, all these things come together to create a real neighborhood."
>
> JOEL SCHIAVONE,
> *New Haven developer*

Our suggestion was to start by looking closely at how the street functioned. We saw several important things right away, including sidewalks that were too narrow to accommodate sidewalk cafes, as they had been narrowed several years before to allow for an extra traffic lane. This unfriendly redesign had also removed parking and therefore increased traffic speeds on the street. The result was that Chapel Street became a thoroughfare, rather than a nice place to stroll and shop. Soon after that redesign, businesses began to suffer and the street began to die.

We proposed a different type of plan—one that would make Chapel Street a real place, not just a street spruced up with a lot of frills. Our approach supported the functions and activities of the street. The sidewalks were restored to their original width at the intersections to allow outdoor dining, and parking spaces were returned to the rest of the block. Trees were strategically located so that they did not block shop windows, and a select few other elements encouraged desirable functions. For instance, two benches, along with a waste receptacle, were situated near a store where people would be likely to wait outside. The result of locating all these elements in relationship to each other was magical: Chapel Street sprang back to life.

"The whole thing is like a mosaic," remarks developer Joel Schiavone, who was instrumental in getting the changes accomplished. "Each piece needs to be carefully considered: street furniture, some flower boxes, a particular tenant for a storefront, tree plantings. If it's done right, all these things come together to create a real neighborhood."

NEW HAVEN'S CHAPEL STREET DURING CONSTRUCTION

NEW HAVEN'S CHAPEL STREET AFTER CONSTRUCTION

A chief goal in planning a public space is to create activity and synergy between the elements in the space and among the people using the space. To achieve this, triangulation —the idea that elements in relationship to each other will stimulate linkages between people and places—is essential.

⑨ Start with the petunias

Placemaking is about doing more than planning. And many great plans get bogged down because they are too big, too expensive, and simply take too long to happen. Short-term actions, like planting petunias, can be a way of not only testing ideas, but also giving people the confidence that change is occurring, and

that their ideas matter. In many of the most successful public spaces, short-term actions occurred at the outset and were evaluated while longer term planning was in progress.

We were working in a downtown park that needed a complete capital restoration to restore its vitality. Since this was an expensive, long-term campaign, a book market was set up in small tent structures around the park's perimeter. This experiment gave confidence to the organization managing the park's restoration, and demonstrated that retail uses would draw people and animate the park. When the park was finally reconstructed several

years later, other types of retail uses were included in its management plan.

John Kotter, a Harvard Business School professor, told us that people who successfully lead a program of change in a corporation or organization always "look for avenues that will allow them to produce some short-term wins, some visible changes that are associated with their effort, within six or 12 months. This gives them credibility and discourages the cynics—and there are always a lot of cynics. Change of any magnitude tends to take time, so short-term wins are essential, and must be an integral part of the long-term strategy." ∎

Case study: Mulry Square, New York, New York

At a dangerous intersection of several streets in New York City, the Department of Transportation and the local community developed a concept for improving the safety of pedestrians. Recommendations made in 1994 included extending the sidewalks at the corners, reconfiguring crosswalks, and adding trees and plants to the area, as well as implementing short–term improvements and experiments like striping in new crosswalks and "havens" for pedestrians with paint, setting out temporary bollards and planters, and changing the timing of traffic lights. Although the city was reluctant to immediately commit to the changes, they agreed to "see" what the results of these temporary measures would be. Evaluations showed a positive effect on pedestrian use of the intersection, as well as on civilizing vehicular traffic in the area. Based on the findings of the experiment, the city is now constructing permanent improvements that include built-up granite paving stones in pedestrian areas, new trees and other plantings, and decorative street lighting. "By experimenting with simple, visible, temporary actions like painting lines in the street, we were able to show the city how larger investment could pay off," said Shirley Secunda, a Community Board member.

> "By experimenting with simple, visible, temporary actions like painting lines in the street, we were able to show the city how larger investment could pay off."
>
> SHIRLEY SECUNDA,
> *Community Board Member*

MULRY SQUARE, NEW YORK CITY (BEFORE)

MULRY SQUARE (AFTER) WHITE STRIPES INDICATED PROPOSED SIDEWALKS AND CROSSWALKS

In creating or changing a public space, small improvements help to garner support along the way to the end result. They indicate visible change and show that someone is in charge. Petunias, which are low cost and easy to plant, have an immediate visible impact. On the other hand, once planted, they must be watered and cared for. Therefore, these flowers give a clear message that someone must be looking after the space.

PALEY PARK, NEW YORK CITY

⑩ Money is not the issue

All too often, lack of money is used as an excuse for doing nothing, which is why this principle harks back to the previously discussed "They always say 'It can't be done.'" In fact, we'd venture to say that too much money might actually discourage the inventiveness and creativity required to create a great place. In these cases, the money is usually just handed to a professional designer, who, it is supposed, "knows better." But no one knows better about what a public space should be like than the people who are using it. When money is the issue, this is generally an indication that the wrong concept is at work—not because the plans are too expensive, but because the public doesn't feel like the place belongs to them.

When money is the issue, this is generally an indication that the wrong concept is at work, not because the plans are too expensive, but because the public doesn't feel like the place belongs to them.

Case study: Albert Park, San Rafael, California

The parks director of a small city in California knew that Albert Park needed improvements. However, money was short. At the same time, a very dedicated and strong community showed great interest in the park. The challenge was to tap its strengths. We helped the parks director to collect data about who was using the park and what their perceptions of the park were. The director discovered issues that ranged from lack of activities in the park to a poor relationship between the senior center, located on the park's edge, and the park itself.

> After forming committees to pursue individual goals, the community used every connection it could muster, receiving in-kind donations and support from myriad local businesses and civic groups.

Concerned citizens came together at a meeting in 1992 to discuss the basic findings of the evaluation. Their ideas included building bocce courts, planting a formal garden, and adding a porch to the senior center to reconnect it with the park. The parks director promised the group that the city would help the community implement its vision, but noted that all parties needed to work together, and contribute.

After forming committees to pursue individual goals, the community used every connection it could muster, receiving in-kind donations and support from myriad local businesses and civic groups. The city had to be extremely flexible in allowing construction to take place, since work was contracted quickly, and a great deal of authority had to be delegated to the community members.

In particular, the bocce courts became a major source of civic pride. Players and their families come nightly from all over San Rafael, with wine, picnics and barbecues. Seniors, who used to frequent the community center but rarely ventured into the park, now have organized a daytime bocce league of their own. Local politicians and city officials hold meetings at the park and show it off to outsiders, while television features, newspaper articles, and a newsletter have attracted bocce enthusiasts from all over the U.S., as well as Europe.

ALBERT PARK, SAN RAFAEL, CALIFORNIA

Four lessons about money and public spaces

- **Small-scale, inexpensive improvements can be more effective at drawing people into spaces than major big-buck projects**, as we note with a previous principle: "Start with the petunias." Inexpensive amenities such as vending carts, outdoor café tables and chairs, umbrellas, flowers, benches, or movable seating are relatively inexpensive. Such items are not generally costly when compared with the overall budget for a public space, but are often eliminated as frills, and as a result, another potential place bites the dust.

- **Developing the ability to effectively manage a space is more critical to success than a large financial investment.** Management is the subject of our final principle, "You are never finished," but it's worth mentioning here that substantial capital investments in spaces do not pay off—good management does. For example, the ability to put out items such as movable furniture at a moment's notice, to host a range of events, or to notice changes in the use of the space and act on them are all ways in which a continuous management presence makes a place successful.

- **If the community is a partner in the endeavor, people will come forward and naturally draw in others.** Principle 3 says that "You can't do it alone," and it is this very mandate that will help you to gather contributions that will make a place grow and thrive. These contributions are not necessarily monetary, but may come in the form of donated goods and services or volunteer labor. Consequently the cost of the project is diminished relative to the benefits received. In neighborhoods throughout the United States, people have, above all odds, salvaged vacant lots and transformed them into significant places in their communities, and continue to gather in them and tend to them. The cost of maintaining these spaces is high in sweat equity, but not dollars.

- **When the community's vision is driving a project, money follows.** Projects perceived by the public as being too expensive often do not become a reality. Why? These types of projects have not evolved from a community's vision. The most successful public space projects tend to use an incremental approach in which the place grows little by little; accordingly, people become more and more invested as it grows. Once a community backs a project with its voices and its hearts, money usually follows. ■

11 **You are never finished**

You probably have already come to the conclusion that creating a great place is not about developing an award-winning design. It is primarily based on a community's vision, and an excellent management plan. We estimate that about 80% of the success of any public space can usually be attributed to its management. No matter how good the design of a space is, it will never become a true place unless it is well managed.

Management is critical because good places are not static—they change daily, weekly, and seasonally. Good management maintains the needed flexibility to deal with those changes. Given the certainty of change and the fluid nature in the use of a place at different times, the challenge is to develop the ability to respond effectively.

Public space management can be done at several different levels, depending not only on the type of public space, but also on the city and region. Some places have paid and staffed management organizations, while others make use of volunteer efforts. In many cities, the private sector has stepped forward to supplement the public sector; with downtown management organizations funded through business improvement districts (BIDs), main street management programs, conservancies, and friends groups.

Case Study: San Bernardino, California

For nearly 20 years, there had been no downtown development in San Bernardino. Then a local businessman became convinced that economic revitalization would never occur without improvements to the downtown environment. Most of the streets of the town were very wide and traffic sped through without stopping. The center of the city, a one-acre site in front of city hall, was a parking lot.

> Without broader, ongoing involvement, the place will not ever develop into a true civic square.

Several community meetings resulted in a vision to create a central square, including a tent for gatherings, in part of the parking lot. Just nine months after the meetings, the square was created simply by planting sod and erecting a temporary tent structure. The square was an instant success, hosting events and activities for many different community groups and welcoming others with a notice about its availability. Enthusiastic responses flowed in. More community meetings were held to develop a second phase in the plan for the square. And because people could see changes downtown, they became vested in the place. The square drew activity downtown and had a major, positive impact on the overall economic climate in San Bernardino.

The townspeople made one critical mistake, however: they thought they were finished. Although a management organization was started, it lost its way and has now withered. There is talk of turning the space over to the parks department. Regular events are still held in the square, but the same community groups run them. Without broader, ongoing involvement, the place will not ever develop into a true civic square.

SAN BERNADINO, CALIFORNIA (BEFORE)

SAN BERNADINO, CALIFORNIA (AFTER)

LUXEMBOURG GARDENS, PARIS, FRANCE

If they are well used, public spaces wear out, and that is good. Anything that people use and love eventually needs to be replaced or repaired. Demands on a place change and being open to the need for change, and having the management flexibility to enact that change, is what builds great public spaces.

IV. Workbook for evaluating public spaces

Contents

1. *Characteristics of A Successful Place*

2. *Understanding How Places Work*

3. *Putting It All Together*

4. *Observational Techniques*

Once you know what to look for, you'll see that there are myriad clues that indicate whether a public place is working or not. We have developed a range of techniques for identifying and interpreting those clues, which range from asking a few relatively simple questions to a conducting a detailed public space audit.

The audit involves visiting the site to observe how people use it and how the physical elements in the space function in relation to those uses. It also involves talking with people who use the place and those who live or work nearby to get a sense of how they view the place. A more complex audit includes evaluating performance data on issues such as real estate values and demographic changes. An empty space is not only less safe than one that people frequent, but it also can detract from and negatively impact adjacent properties.

Numerous variables make it impossible to rate a space in terms of absolute numbers of people who use it. Size, time of day and year,

LIBERTY STATE PARK, JERSEY CITY, NEW JERSEY

amount and location of seating, events and activities, and other factors all impact what could be considered the "correct" number of people for any space. It is safe to say, however, that if a place feels empty and uncomfortable, there are too few people; and if it feels comfortable and busy but not too crowded, it has the right number. The main point is to remember that a successful public place is used, and a space that is not working is empty, or has been taken over by negative uses. Public space evaluations can be done easily by anyone who is observant, from a highly trained professional to a layperson. Both can achieve dramatic results. ■

① Characteristics of a Successful Place

In his studies of plazas 30 years ago, William H. Whyte identified many of the key indicators of good public places, brilliantly described in his book, *The Social Life of Small Urban Spaces*, and in his documentary, "City Places/City Spaces." Knowledge of Whyte's basic findings is essential to anyone who evaluates a public space. One of them is: "What attracts people, it would appear, is other people." Therefore, a central question in evaluating any space is, "What is it that attracted the first person?" Luckily, those things are easily identified, and include: places to sit; plenty of shade; "touchable" water; good food, and well-connected streets and sidewalks.

The specific characteristics of a successful place are:

High proportion of people in groups

LUXEMBOURG GARDENS, PARIS, FRANCE

The presence of people in groups can be an index of selectivity. Whyte's Street Life Project found that often when people go to a plaza in twos or threes, or always when they rendezvous there, it is because they have decided to do so in advance.

Higher than average proportion of women

BROOKLYN, NEW YORK

Women tend to be more discriminating about the spaces that they use. Reasons for this range from women's choosiness when it comes to the types of seating available in a place, to their perceptions about whether a place is safe.

Different ages

The presence of different ages usually means a place has different constituencies who use it at different times of day. For example, pre-school age children and their guardians can use a neighborhood park when others are working, as can seniors and retirees.

GRANVILLE ISLAND, VANCOUVER, CANADA

Varied activities

Popular places generally have more things to do than less successful spaces. And activities don't necessarily require special equipment or facilities.

GREENWICH VILLAGE, NEW YORK CITY

Affection

PARIS, FRANCE

There is generally more smiling, kissing, embracing, holding and shaking of hands, and so forth in good public places than in those that are problematic.

② Understanding How Places Work

The Place Diagram provides a framework for evaluating how a space is "performing."

In this section you'll find a series of questions to consider based on each section of the Place Diagram—Access and Linkage, Uses and Activities, Comfort and Image and Sociability—that are easy to use as an evaluation or audit of a particular place. In turn, these questions lead us to identify typical visible signs of problems, also based on the Diagram, that indicate how a space is performing. We have also suggested several techniques that are useful in understanding a particular issue better, many of which are described in the final section of this handbook. Finally, we have listed a few ways of improving the space.

How to Turn a Place Around

Sociability

Uses & Activities

Place

Access & Linkage

Comfort & Image

Uses and Activities

Questions to consider

- Are people using the space or is it empty?

- Is it used by a range of ages?

- Do people cluster in groups? What kinds of groups—couples, friends, co-workers, families, multigenerational families, small or large groups?

- How many types of activities are occurring—for example, are people walking, eating, relaxing, reading and playing baseball, or chess?

- Which parts of the space are used and which are not? Are there noticeable patterns—for example, are elderly people using the benches; small children clustered around the swings; teenagers hanging out around the entrance?

- Is it easy to go from part of the space to another?

- How does the overall design relate to people's use of the space? For example, are entrances and paths, benches and waste receptacles made convenient?

BRYANT PARK, NEW YORK CITY

- Are there obvious choices of things to do? Are events and activities being held, or made evident by a schedule? Who is responsible for the events? How does the design of the space relate to events that are held there?

- Is there a management presence? Can you identify that anyone is in charge of the space?

Visible signs of problems

- The space is empty of people for all or part of the day.

- The space is congested because it is too small for the number of people present.

- There is a lack of places to sit.

- There is a lack of gathering points—activities are isolated from each other, there are no focal points.

- The space does not accommodate events very well.

Suggested ways of measuring activity

- Record the number and type of activities at different times of the day and week.

- Survey people in the community or people in the place about their perceptions of the place and what they would like to see there in the future.

- Take an inventory of adjacent land uses (e.g. the presence of a school, church, library, or office building, etc.) to determine activities that would attract people but are missing.

Ways of improving the space

- Provide amenities that will support desired activities.

- Create focal points where people will gather.

- Develop a series of community oriented programs with local talent from institutions (churches, schools, libraries, farmers market, etc.) to attract people in the short term and to demonstrate that someone is in charge.

- Change the types of events that are held or modify the space, if necessary, to better accommodate events.

- Work with adjacent property owners and retailers to develop strategies to lease ground floors of empty buildings and help revitalize the area.

Comfort and Image

Questions to Consider

- Does the place make a good first impression?

- Are there more women than men?

- Are there enough places to sit? Are seats conveniently located? Do people have a choice of places to sit, either in the sun or shade? Is appropriate weather protection (umbrellas, shelters) offered?

- Is there a management presence or is it apparent that anyone is in charge of the space? Are spaces clean and free of litter? Who is responsible for maintenance? What do they do? When?

- Does the area feel safe? Is there a security presence? If so, what do these people do? When are they on duty?

- Are people are taking pictures? Are there many photo opportunities available?

- Do vehicles dominate pedestrian use of the space, or prevent them from easily getting to the space?

LUXEMBOURG GARDENS, PARIS, FRANCE

Women are bellwethers for a successful place because they are much more discriminating about the types of public spaces they choose to use. Therefore, a good place will generally have a higher proportion of women than men. Women vote with both their feet and with their intuition: For example, their perceptions about safety affect their decision to use a place, as do elements like the height or texture of seating and the types of other people present.

Visible signs of problems

- There are too few places to sit.

- No one appears to be in charge.

- The space is unattractive or feels unsafe.

- Litter and other signs of poor maintenance are evident.

- "Undesirables" are able to dominate the space.

- Security problems are evident: broken windows, graffiti, vandalism, etc.

- The space is dominated by vehicles.

Suggested ways to measure comfort and image

- Record your first impressions carefully, ask other people to do the same (particularly those who have never been to the space before), and compare notes. You can never be a first-timer more than once.

- Review crime statistics and complaints.

- Survey people's perceptions about an area regarding safety, attractiveness, cleanliness, etc.

- Observe the use of amenities such as seating.

- Track people to and within the space to identify circulation problems.

Ways to improve a place's comfort and image

- Add amenities—seating, telephones, waste receptacles, information booths, food vendors, community-oriented public art, flowers, fountains—in carefully considered locations.

- Create a management presence through vendors or food/information kiosks, by creating an entrance or adding a view onto the place from windows in an adjacent building. This requires creative thinking.

- Increase security by providing more uses for and activities at the place, or by appointing someone to be in charge of it. Upgrade maintenance, including daily cleaning and preventative maintenance of physical facilities. Establish a community policing program.

Access and Linkages

Questions to Consider

- Can you see the space from a distance? Is the interior of the place visible from the outside?

- Can people easily walk to the place (e.g. they aren't darting between moving cars to get to and from the bus stop to the park)?

- Do sidewalks lead to and from adjacent areas, allowing for convenient pedestrian access?

- Does the space function for people with special needs? Is it ADA compliant?

- Do the roads and paths through the space match with where people want to go?

- Do occupants of adjacent buildings use the space?

- Do a variety of transportation options provide access to the place? (e.g. bus, train, car, and bicycle.)

SARATOGA SPRINGS, NEW YORK

Visible signs of problems

- Traffic is congested or fast moving, and is a barrier to pedestrians crossing the street.

- Bicycles are infrequently used as a way of access.

- People are walking in the street or wearing paths through areas not paved as sidewalks (such as lawns, planted beds, etc.).

- Pedestrian-oriented uses (such as storefronts) are discontinuous, creating an unpleasant walking environment.

- There is insufficient parking.

Ways of measuring access

- Conduct observations, counts, and tracking of pedestrian circulation within and around a place.

- Record the location and finish treatment of sidewalks and number of curb cuts to determine suitability for walking.

- Map the area (to determine which uses generate pedestrian activity).

- Survey pedestrians to determine attitudes and patterns.

- Survey the broader community to determine how and why different modes of transportation are used.

- Conduct parking turnover studies to determine efficiency of use.

- Conduct traffic studies to determine level of use over the day and week, as well as occupancy of vehicles.

Ways of improving the accessibility of the space

- Widen sidewalks or provide sidewalk extensions at crosswalks, better balancing pedestrian uses with other uses (vehicles, transit vehicles, bicycles, deliveries, etc.).

- Construct more clearly marked or more conveniently located crosswalks.

- Make accommodations for bicycle users (bike lanes, lockers, storage racks, etc.).

- Infill vacant lots with structures and uses to create continuity of pedestrian experience.

- Balance on-street parking with other uses.

- Change traffic signal timing to improve pedestrian access.

- Improve use of parking through changes in enforcement or regulation.

Sociability

Questions to Consider

- Is this a place where you would choose to meet your friends? Are other people meeting their friends here or running into friends?

- Do people come in groups?

- Are people talking with each other?

- Are people smiling?

- Do people seem to use the place (or facility) regularly and by choice?

- Do users know each other by face or by name?

- Do people bring their friends and relatives to see the place or do they point to one of the elements with pride?

- Do strangers make eye contact with each other?

- Is there is a mix of ages and ethnic groups that generally reflects the community at large?

- Do people tend to pick up litter when they see it?

LAGUNA BEACH, CALIFORNIA

Visible signs of problems

- People do not interact with other users of the place.

- There is a lack of diversity of people using a place.

Ways of measuring sociability

- Survey people about their perceptions of a place.

- Identify the number of people and local associations or organizations who volunteer to help or just assume responsibility for a particular area.

Ways of improving the sociability of the space

- Develop focal points—public gathering places that accommodate a variety of activities.

- Arrange amenities to encourage social interaction (grouping benches, moveable seating, etc.).

- Stage special events and activities to draw people.

- Encourage community volunteers to assist with improvements or maintenance of a place.

- Provide a variety of uses in adjacent buildings to attract a diversity of people.

3 Putting it all together

The issues outlined above are to be used as a guide as you look at a place; they should give you a sense of how it rates and help you to decide which types of additional data collection are required.

What follows are the key steps that we think are useful in getting more people involved in a place, and then determining the types of improvements that need to be made there. Several of the steps can be undertaken as part of a community-based visioning process, during which community members identify issues, contribute ideas, help collect data, and collaborate on solutions. Because every situation is different, the steps are not always exactly the same. However, the general flow of the process involves: consulting with the community at the outset; making observations and collecting data at the place in order to discover and substantiate its critical issues; presenting those issues to the community for additional input; and finally, implementing the community's vision.

Community-based process

1. **Meet with community representatives from both public and private sectors to identify the range of issues that various groups face regarding a particular place.** If the area of concern is a downtown street, for instance, the issues will likely include: pedestrian/vehicle conflicts, speed or volume of traffic, lack of appropriate parking, lack of pedestrian access, poorly functioning public transit facilities and transit related amenities such as seating, shelters, etc. In a park, the issues would likely include: inconveniently located amenities such as benches, picnic areas, and waste receptacles; poor maintenance; lack of management presence; increasing park use by providing additional events and attractions.

2. **Formulate hypotheses about issues that merit further data collection and develop a workplan.** By drawing on the questions outlined in the previous section, you can form initial hypotheses about a place. For example: nobody goes there anymore; there's not enough parking; there's nothing

COMMUNITY MEETING, SAN BERNADINO, CALIFORNIA

going on there; it has become a hangout for undesirables. Then decisions must be made regarding the best ways to collect the necessary data to support those hypotheses. The methods are many and varied, ranging from a simple "place performance evaluation" (a one-half to one-day workshop developed by PPS) to more detailed analyses of the use of a place and peoples' perceptions about it. By carefully reading the techniques described in the following section, "Observation Techniques, Surveys and Interviews" you can develop a plan for what kind of evaluation you want to undertake.

3. **Collect on-site data.** The goal of data collection is to understand more fully how a place functions over time. Methods for collecting data about a place include interviews and surveys, as well as observation techniques conducted at sample times of day and week, such as behavior mapping, counts, parking analysis, and tracking. Where appropriate, time-lapse photography can be used to understand general patterns of use such as parking turnover and pedestrian crossing patterns. Often we have enlisted the help of community volunteers to help collect data. For example, in Belmont Shores, California, business people and residents recorded parking turnover and also set up tables along the street to distribute surveys to shoppers, while in Red Hook, Brooklyn, residents distributed surveys to their neighbors. Several large business-

es in Detroit (including a computer software company) distributed surveys and collected ideas from employees, and the mayor's office presented the results on a web site. In Austin, Texas, residents made the place performance evaluation a central part of a one-day workshop they organized.

4. **Analyze data, review community input, and identify potential ideas for implementation.** The steps below will help you to use the data that you collect to formulate an action plan. Because there are many different solutions to the same problem, this task is significantly easier if you have spent time in the place yourself, doing at least some of the observations and interviews. Basic tips for analyzing data include:

- Consolidate data and create summaries of all results. Some of the results can be graphed; others can be written summaries of notes.

- Compare data to the hypotheses you made at the outset and form new hypotheses.

- Outline all major findings. These should be grouped into logical categories related to the issues concerning a place: access and circulation, maintenance, programs and events, security, etc.

- Relate each finding to a recommendation that will help solve the issue. It's helpful to think of your findings as problems and your recommendations as solutions.

5. Conduct a public forum for community representatives and interested members of the larger community. Review the data that has been collected, further define issues, and encourage input about improvements and ideas for improvements. Brainstorm ideas further in small focus groups, which can then become committees that address specific issues. We have found that using slides to illustrate the issues in a place, along with examples of how other cities are handling similar issues, helps to stimulate new thinking, encourage ongoing participation, and—because it has been done elsewhere—build confidence in the community's ideas.

6. Translate data into a conceptual plan. Once the findings and recommendations have been organized, reviewed, and added to by the community, it's fairly easy to develop a conceptual plan. The plan can include written materials as well as graphic representations of ideas. It may or may not be possible to determine how much the recommendations will cost at this point, which skills might be needed, and which types of partners should be involved.

For example, a straightforward problem such as a poorly maintained plaza can often be dealt with by simply increasing the number of times the waste recep-

Tips for Conducting Community Meetings

1. Acknowledge the timing and seriousness of the issue. For example, controversial projects that are perceived as a threat to the quality of life in a neighborhood will draw good attendance at a community meeting. In situations where a place-oriented approach is being used, it may be necessary to initiate the process on a very small scale—in people's living rooms, for instance, or at a downtown business.

2. Choose a meeting place that is convenient for the community. This helps to ensure a good turnout. For example, a meeting about a proposal to build a community center in a park should be held in the park if possible, or in a building directly adjacent to it. If the meeting is in city hall, or an official place set apart from the community, it probably will not be nearly as well attended.

3. Choose a convenient time. If the meeting mainly concerns residents of an area, evening is best, whereas a time right after work is better for meetings about a downtown plaza or park in which businesses are involved.

4. Provide food and beverages. Food and drink is a sure attraction, especially if the meeting is held during a mealtime. It also helps create a comfortable atmosphere and can get strangers talking to one another.

tacles are emptied, or the way the space is managed. Generally, however, problems with a place are more difficult, such as finding ways to discourage certain types of uses in a place, while simultaneously encouraging more positive uses. Dealing with these issues is a more complex undertaking, one that requires familiarity with specific issues in the place, as well as a broader understanding of the relationship between the use, physical elements, and management of public places.

7. **Refine and discuss recommendations, and develop an implementation plan.** Ideally this should be done with community representatives. The plan should include an estimated budget; responsibilities for partners, local community organizations, and the private sector; and a schedule. Because communities are generally very action-oriented, a variety of short-term demonstration projects will likely result, incorporating changes in both the physical place and its management.

Even though government agencies tend to move more slowly, it is important that they respect the benefits of short-term wins, which build momentum for a project and keep the community involved. The good news is that many of the solutions will be comparatively low in cost and can be quickly implemented— if the public sector can develop the necessary flexibility.

④ Observation Techniques

Methods of collecting information about a public place are as varied as the places themselves. This section provides in-depth descriptions of several observational techniques—such as trace measures, behavior mapping, counting, and tracking—as well as techniques for measuring people's perceptions, including interviews and questionnaires. Each description includes information on when and how to use a technique, and an example of a form that can be used to collect the information. These techniques can be used in many different ways-over an hour or two, or for longer periods of time. However, observations should never be conducted just once. They should be done over several different periods, on a weekday and weekend, at night and in the morning, afternoon or evening, to better understand the "flow" of a place. You may be surprised at what you discover.

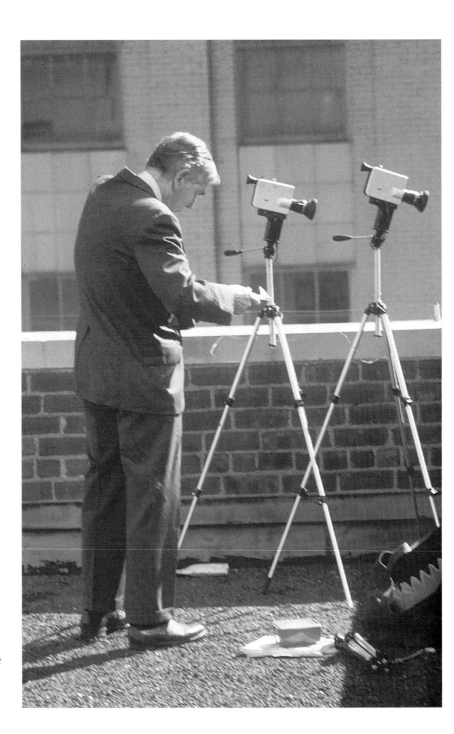

William H. Whyte mastered the art of observing public spaces to determine how successful they were. He liked to remind us that simple things, though seemingly obvious, are often ignored.

Behavior Mapping

Behavior mapping, also known as activity mapping, allows you to study people's activities in a specific area for a predetermined amount of time. Stationary activities such as sunbathing, sitting, leaning, talking, and reading can be documented, as can activities involving motion: walking, jogging, biking, etc.

When to use this technique

Behavior mapping is one of the most valuable tools for making informed decisions about both about the placement and design of various facilities and for changes in management practices. Behavior maps can show, for example, that a picnic area next to a playground is always heavily used, while another picnic area is seldom used.

Insights gained through this focused and regular process of recording information are invaluable; however, one must be careful to systematically collect the data (e.g. during different times of day, week, etc.) so that all types of activities are represented, creating a comprehensive picture of the use of a place. For example, although a jogging path may seem adequate and free of problems at one time of the day, observations at other times may reveal bicyclists and joggers competing for the same space. It is also critical that all observers be trained to record information correctly and consistently. If an observer forgets to record the number of teenagers at a pool or the cars parked along the road, it will invalidate his or her data, and that of the other observers.

A behavior mapping form has two parts: a map of the area and space to record information about the activities and types of people. The map should include trees, facilities, seating, fountains, and any other prominent features in the place. A separate form is required for each period of observation.

How to map behavior

Determine the kind of information needed and whether it is necessary to record activity in the entire place or only in specific areas. This decision depends on the purpose of the mapping. For example, if the purpose were to gain a general understanding of problems in a space, the entire space would be mapped; however, if, say, a playground within the space is to be redesigned, only that area need be observed.

Behavior mapping can record both stationary people and those in motion. However, since people moving through a place are often too numerous or moving too fast, information about them is best recorded through counting. Mapping is most valuable when limited to stationary people.

Some activities, such as socializing, are often done in conjunction with specific activities such as picnicking. For this reason, it is important to decide on the types of activities that will be recorded, their definition, and whether to check off more than one activity per person observed.

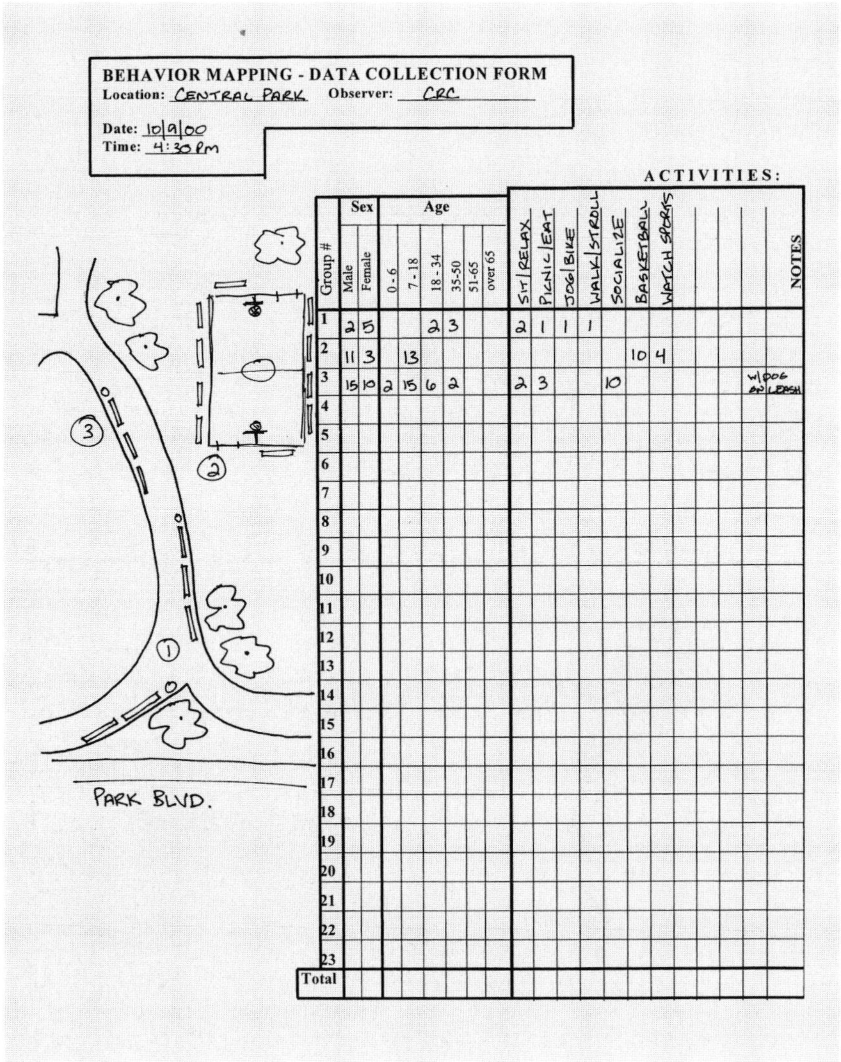

BEHAVIOR MAPPING - DATA COLLECTION FORM

Location: CENTRAL PARK **Observer:** CRC

Date: 10/9/00

Time: 4:30 PM

ACTIVITIES:

Group #	Sex: Male	Female	Age: 0-6	7-18	18-34	35-50	51-65	over 65	SIT/RELAX	PICNIC/EAT	JOG/BIKE	WALK/STROLL	SOCIALIZE	BASKETBALL	WATCH SPORTS					NOTES
1	2	5			2	3			2	1	1	1								
2	11	3		13										10	4					
3	15	10	2	15	6	2			2	3			10							W/DOG ON LEASH
4																				
5																				
6																				
7																				
8																				
9																				
10																				
11																				
12																				
13																				
14																				
15																				
16																				
17																				
18																				
19																				
20																				
21																				
22																				
23																				
Total																				

FIGURE 1: SAMPLE BEHAVIOR MAPPING FORM

How to conduct observations

Stand at one end of the place to be mapped and fill in both the information on the top of the form and all of the activities taking place. For example, if the observer sees two women over 65 are eating and socializing, he or she writes the number "2" under the "female" column, the number "2" under the appropriate age column, and checks the activity or activities in which they are engaged: sitting, eating, socializing. It is important to mark the precise location of the person or group on the map and indicate their relationship to any physical element on the map (e.g. sitting on a bench versus sitting on grass).

The time it takes to map activities varies according to the number of people using the area and the amount of information needed-it may take up to a half-hour to complete an activity map. A reasonable time is 10 to 20 minutes, which allows time between mapping for other observations or interviews. Behavior mapping is usually conducted six or more times a day at regular intervals. In a space with little activity, record everything that occurs over a period of time. For example, for 10 minutes record all of the people who use that area of the space (say, a bench or bus stop). If multiple observers are doing activity mapping at one time in different spaces, the information needs to be recorded in a consistent manner so that it can be compared.

**BEHAVIOR MAPPING
FINAL SUMMARY FORM**

Date: 10/9/00

locatn #	total in groups	total indiv	people alone		SEX male		female		AGE 0-6		7-18		19-60		60+		ACTIVITIES (#/% OF GROUPS) SIT		EAT		JOG		WALK		SOCIAL.		BBALL		WATCH							
			#	%	#	%	#	%	#	%	#	%	#	%	#	%	#	%	#	%	#	%	#	%	#	%	#	%	#	%	#	%	#	%
1	160	210	110	52	89	42	121	58	25	12	31	15	142	67	12	6	150	94	40	25	60	38	75	47	8	5	10	6	3	2				
2	172	251	122	48	109	43	142	57	16	5	34	14	172	69	29	12	172	100	71	41	63	36	9	5	112	65	5	3	—	—				
3	154	175	101	57	75	43	100	57	4	2	5	3	158	90	8	5	149	97	78	51	74	48	27	19	10	6	—	—	—	—				
Total	486	636	333	52	273	42	363	57	45	7	70	11	472	74	49	7	471	74	189	30	197	31	111	17	130	20	15	2	3	1				

FIGURE 2: SAMPLE SUMMARY FORM

Once a place has been fully recorded onto a series of activity maps, it's time to analyze the results of the collected data. First, totals must be counted up at the bottom of each form; then the data should be consolidated onto a form that totals the locations and activities together. Finally, one must come to some conclusions about how the results relate to the project. For example, if the project is to make revisions in a maintenance schedule to make a place cleaner and more attractive, the relevant information from activity mapping would concern what parts of the space are used or not used, at what times of day, and the types of activities that occur in different areas. Using this information, one could then develop a new schedule for maintenance that would identify where, when, and what kinds of additional cleaning and repair are needed for each area.

Counting

Counting is a systematic method of gathering numerical data about people, vehicles or anything else in a specific location or passing a particular point.

When to use this technique

Counts can be used to determine such things as vehicles' use of streets, or the number of people who enter a place at a particular point, or whether a particular bikepath, which may seem crowded, actually is crowded. In addition, counts can be useful in identifying specific issues beyond just volume (e.g. the percentage of people over the age of 60). Counts can provide significant information only when comparisons are made. For example, the total number of women in a place becomes significant only if compared with the number of men, or the number of women in a place at one time of day versus another.

How to conduct counts

Decide what you want to count. If traffic is heavy, such as on a busy street, you may only be able to count how many cars or people cross a certain point over a given time period. However, if traffic is lighter, such as on a park path or greenway, the counting form below can be amended to allow the counter to also account for the types of activities being counted. This can be useful depending on the issues you have identified. Counts on a greenway or path may be of bicyclists, skateboarders, in-line skaters, joggers, walkers, people with strollers, etc.

Decide on the length and frequency of the counting periods. This decision depends on what is being counted and how long it will take to get a representative sample. For example, if people on a shopping street are being counted, you might decide to count how many people walk past a certain landmark over a six-minute period. Then the

---

PEDESTRIAN COUNT FORM

Date: 11/1/86
Location: MAIN STREET
Duration of Count: 12 MIN.
Observer: SD

TIME	DIRECTION EAST		DIRECTION WEST		TOTAL
9:00	HH HH HH HH IIII	24	HH HH I	11	35
10:00	HH HH HH HH HH I	26	HH HH I	11	37
11:00	HH HH HH HH HH	25	HH HH I	11	36
12:00	HH HH HH HH HH II	27	HH HH III	13	40
1:00	HH HH HH HH	20	HH HH II	12	32
2:00	HH HH II	12	HH III	8	20
3:00	HH HH HH HH I	21	HH HH III	13	34
4:00	HH HH HH HH	20	HH HH II	12	32

FIGURE 3: SAMPLE COUNTING FORM

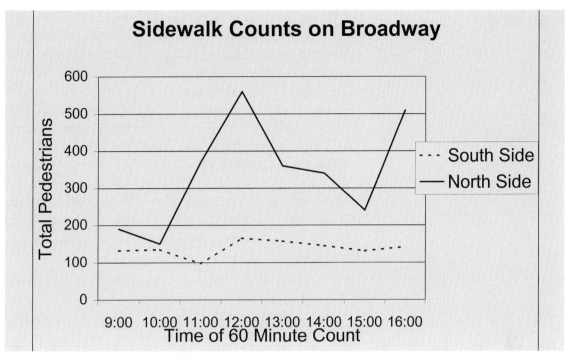

FIGURE 4

number can be multiplied by 10 to determine approximately how many people walk down that side of the street in an hour. One "rule of thumb" is that a street must have at least 1,000 people per hour walking on it to support retail.

Analyze the Data. Once the numbers have been tallied, the totals may be graphed or charted to understand or clarify specific points. For example, the total number of people walking down Broadway may be graphed over time and thus clarify high and low points in its use (see Figure 4), or the number of people who use different paths through a plaza over the summer may be charted. These data are then used to make recommendations. Data concerning the use of a roadway may convince a traffic department to introduce parking on the street, or eliminate a lane that can then be used as sidewalk space.

Data concerning paths may be used in developing signage or facilities at certain points, or in decisions to widen a path or build others. Counts are valuable in situations where "hard" data is required, both to understand a problem and to communicate information to others.

The most difficult part of analyzing counts is to fit them into the context of the overall findings and recommendations for a space. Used alone, counts are often meaningless, but used in comparison with other counts or other types of data they become very important.

Tracking

Tracking is a simple observation technique in which the observer follows visitors into and through a place, to learn more about how the place is used and about circulation into and through it.

When to use this technique

Tracking is useful for learning the routes people take from one location to another, for defining which paths through a place are most heavily used, and for understanding how people cross a street. It is useful only when movement through an area is an issue. For example, if a problem is that the stalls on the left aisle of a farmers market are not as heavily used as those on the right, tracking can determine where people turn after entering the market. Tracking is also good for analyzing jaywalking patterns (see figure 5).

TRACKING DATA COLLECTION FORM

LOCATION _COOPER SQUARE_

TIME BEGIN _7:30 Am_   TIME END _8:30 Am_

OBSERVER _CC_

FIGURE 5: SAMPLE TRACKING FORM NOTING WHERE PEOPLE CROSS THE STREET.

VIEW OF INTERSECTION "TRACKED" IN
FIGURE 5 (LEFT)

Tracking reveals how frequently both paths and various destination points are used, making it very useful for planning purposes. Detailed information also can be obtained on stopping-off points, or even people's comments about specific problems, if their conversations are noted.

Tracking is not difficult but it does demand concentration and attention. Its limitations are that it does not easily allow you to discover potential issues or problems on the site; therefore, it should be used only when you are certain that the information you will get is valuable to the questions at hand.

How to track

Tracking is relatively simple, and can be done in two ways. One way is to select a spot that allows a good view of the location(s) to be studied. Stand there and watch people, and then record on one map where they go (see figure 5). When the paths are recorded in this manner, patterns become evident. For example, you may need to observe the entrance and destination point in a plaza in order to determine if the majority of people who entered it at various entrances all exited primarily at one point. The second way to track is to actually follow people. This is useful if you cannot identify a vantage point from which you can witness people's entire route through an area. Once the data is analyzed, decisions can be made as to which paths can be strengthened through design improvements, which can be eliminated, and what new paths should be added.

Trace Measures

When people use a place, they leave traces. These usually fall into two categories: physical evidence and erosion traces. Physical evidence includes objects people leave behind, such as beer cans and other litter. Beer cans found in a corner of a place in the morning suggest how it was used the previous evening. Litter that accumulates during a specific time (e.g., lunch hour) can indicate the degree to which a plaza is used during that time. The type of litter (soda cans or Perrier bottles) can also sometimes provide evidence of the type of people who have eaten lunch there. Erosion traces are signs of wear, both obvious and hidden, found on the surfaces of the ground, walls, furniture, handrails, etc. A path worn across a lawn is evidence that many people have taken a short cut along that route. Worn steps, handrails polished smooth, and paint worn off walls all indicate patterns of use.

When to use this technique

Recording traces is a good way of understanding activities that are not readily apparent through observations. It should be done early on and is particularly useful in suggesting hypotheses about a place. Traces can be recorded quantitatively (e.g. the number of cans or the volume of litter) and qualitatively (e.g. no trace of wear, or lightly-moderately-heavily worn). This information can be extremely helpful in building a case for specific improvements such as additional trash receptacles, introducing a recycling program, or redesigning plaza pathways.

Overflowing trash cans and excessive debris indicate how people use a park, as well as other issues.

How to record traces

Traces only need to be recorded sporadically, and are done by writing down observations either on a map or on paper that is coded to correspond to areas on a map. Once a day, once a week, or even once a month may be enough, depending on the kind of information being recorded. One may, for example, record changes in the amount of litter in receptacles at different times throughout the day, or annually record the apparent "wear" effect of use on play equipment.

Paths worn through the grass, sometimes called desire lines, indicate how people want to use a space.

Interviews and Questionnaires

Interviews and questionnaires measure the attitudes, perceptions, and motivations that cannot be obtained from observing people's behavior. As with observations, different methods yield different types of results.

An informal interview is simply a conversation; often it relates to the activity of the interviewee, or may arise spontaneously from any issue. Informal interviews are generally not used to obtain numerical data, but rather to find out how people perceive or use a place. In documenting responses, it is important to try to record, either on paper or on audiotape, the exact words and phrases people use.

A guided interview is a more structured method in which the interviewer has a series of questions or topics on issues that need to be explored. Regardless of the interview's length, information obtained from each person should be comparable. The guided interview is very flexible: the interviewer can rephrase questions and ask additional questions to further explore the interviewee's thoughts about a particular topic.

A questionnaire or survey requires questions that are carefully phrased, ordered, and are not subject to alteration. Multiple-choice questions are often included, followed by probing questions that allow for a more personal amplification of particular points. Multiple-choice questions can be easily analyzed and are simpler to record than

Interviewing Tips

A good interviewer is a good conversationalist: He or she has interest in others, a comfortable relationship with strangers, and an ability to put people at ease. The interviewer should be alert to changes in people's tone and how they respond to different questions. Body language, tone of voice, and facial expressions are "readable" cues that amplify the respondent's verbal messages. For example, although the mother of a small child may answer, "yes" to a question about whether a playground should be expanded, the interviewer may detect doubt in her tone of voice that this is really the best solution. The interviewer should then inquire if perhaps she has another suggestion to improve the playground.

When conducting interviews, it is advisable to always carry identification. In addition, a brief statement typed on official stationery defining the purpose of the research and giving the interview's name will help to dispel suspicions about the legitimacy of the interview.

open-ended ones; open-ended questions, such as "What other kinds of activities would you like to see here?" allow people to give ideas, which can be helpful in formulating new plans for the place.

The types of questions asked in both interviews and questionnaires generally fall into three categories: (1) use (who uses the space, how often, when they tend to use it, and why); (2) attitudes, opinions, and problems regarding the space; and (3) suggestions and ideas on how to improve the space.

It is often helpful to give the respondent a copy of the survey so that he or she can read along as the questions are being asked, especially if English is not the primary language and a translated copy can be provided. (Obviously, it helps immensely if the interviewer speaks more than one language as well.)

The second method involves distributing surveys either to all of the people in one location, or to a

predetermined sample. The observer then picks up the completed surveys a short time later. This method works well with people in groups (e.g. a family picnicking). The observer hands out surveys to all adult members of the group, and when the forms are picked up, the observer randomly selects one questionnaire for analysis as representative of the group. If the group is very large, two forms may be selected for analysis. Keep all group questionnaires together in case perceptions between members of a group are to be evaluated.

Deciding on the most appropriate method depends on the type of space, how many users and activities it has, the number of interviews required, and the length of the questionnaire. For example, a stationary table is probably the most suitable in a downtown plaza used by office employees at lunchtime, or along a walking path; whereas in a spread-out picnic area for example,

Tips for preparing questionnaires

1. *Use simple language.* Avoid technical terms unless the respondents are part of a specialized professional group.

2. *Avoid embarrassing, potentially embarrassing, ambiguous and leading questions.* The first question should be attention getting but not controversial; it must not antagonize anyone. It should be interesting enough to arouse curiosity but must be easy to answer. For example: "How did you get downtown today?" Ambiguous questions can result in answers that are hard to interpret. For example, a question such as "What do you like and dislike about this plaza?" will generate responses that are too varied to be compared meaningfully. It is better to ask people's attitudes toward specific facilities or features in a place.

3. *Leading questions* such as: "Do you think it is safe for children to play in the playground between Main Street and Oak Street?" suggest a particular answer, such as the playground is not safe, or its safety should be questioned. A less biased way of asking the question might be to include it as part of a series of questions regarding overall safety in public spaces.

4. *Develop questions that will help in making design and/or management recommendations* such as "Do you use the playground?" followed by "What piece of equipment do you use the most?" are specifically related to making changes, whereas "How do you feel about the playground?" is not in itself helpful.

5. *Cluster questions on a single topic and ask the general and easier questions before the more specific ones.* The questions should have a logical progression from simple to complex, from impersonal to personal, and should draw and maintain the interest of the person being interviewed.

   More difficult questions should be asked toward the middle of the questionnaire, after the person has become involved but before he or she becomes tired. If sensitive questions are included (e.g. on issues such as drug dealing), they should be positioned toward the end of the questionnaire. At the end, people should be asked for any further comments or suggestions and thanked for their cooperation.

or a bus station, the interviewer will have to move around to distribute the forms or ask the questions. With a smaller number of observers it's possible to obtain more interviews by handing out forms, but this must be weighed against the loss of the important experience of actually talking to people. If several locations or places are being studied, keep the method of collecting information consistent.

In using any of these methods, the selection of a random and representative sample is necessary. The aim is not always to get as many people as possible to respond, but rather to get a representative sample of people. This must include people who use the space at all times of the day-from early-morning to late-night users, and those engaged in its entire range of activities.

In some situations, it is preferable to have people fill out the survey on the spot.

Appendix: Behavior Mapping Forms

BEHAVIOR MAPPING - DATA COLLECTION FORM
Location: _____ Observer: _____

Date: _____
Time: _____

ACTIVITIES:

Group #	Sex		Age																	NOTES
	Male	Female	0 - 6	7 - 18	18 - 34	35-50	51-65	over 65												
1																				
2																				
3																				
4																				
5																				
6																				
7																				
8																				
9																				
10																				
11																				
12																				
13																				
14																				
15																				
16																				
17																				
18																				
19																				
20																				
21																				
22																				
23																				
Total																				

BEHAVIOR MAPPING
FINAL SUMMARY FORM

Date: _____

locatn #	total groups	total indiv	people alone		male		female		0-6		7-18		19-60		60+																			
			#	%	#	%	#	%	#	%	#	%	#	%	#	%	#	%	#	%	#	%	#	%	#	%	#	%	#	%	#	%	#	%

SEX | AGE | ACTIVITIES (#/% OF GROUPS)

Total

Bibliography

Jacobs, Jane, *The Death and Life of Great American Cities*, Vintage Books, New York, 1961.

Kotter, John P., *Leading Change*, Harvard Business School Press, Boston, 1996.

LaFarge, Albert, editor, *The Essential William H. Whyte*, Fordham University Press, New York, 2000.

McKnight, John, and John P. Kretzmann, *Building Communities from the Inside Out*, Acta Publications, Chicago, 1997.

Whyte, William H., *City: Rediscovering the Center*, Anchor Books, New York,1988. (out of print)

Whyte, William H., *The Social Life of Small Urban Spaces*, Project for Public Spaces, Inc. New York, 1980.

For information on PPS's services, placemaking resources, and other publications, visit us online at:

WWW.PPS.ORG

OR CONTACT US AT:
Project for Public Spaces
700 Broadway, 4th floor
New York, NY 10003
(212) 620-5660
pps@pps.org

"Never doubt that a small group of thoughtful, committed citizens can change that world; indeed, it's the only thing that ever has." MARGARET MEAD